A Girl's Guide to College

Life, Guys, & Career

GABRIELLE FANELLI

WESTBOW
PRESS®
A DIVISION OF THOMAS NELSON
& ZONDERVAN

Scripture quotations marked (MSG) are taken from THE MESSAGE. Copyright © by Eugene H. Peterson 1993, 1994, 1995, 1996, 2000, 2001, 2002. Used by permission of NavPress. All rights reserved. Represented by Tyndale House Publishers, Inc.

WestBow Press books may be ordered through booksellers or by contacting:

WestBow Press
A Division of Thomas Nelson & Zondervan
1663 Liberty Drive
Bloomington, IN 47403
www.westbowpress.com
1 (866) 928-1240

ISBN: 978-1-5127-4954-0 (sc)
ISBN: 978-1-5127-4955-7 (hc)
ISBN: 978-1-5127-4953-3 (e)

Library of Congress Control Number: 2016911545

Print information available on the last page.

WestBow Press rev. date: 07/18/2016

Dedication

I dedicate this book to my mom for sacrificing every ounce of yourself to help me become who I am today. You are my best friend. To my dad, thank you for setting the standards high on finding a guy and having an amazing marriage. Thank you for working hard to support our family and helping me reach my dreams. To my brother, your sweet spirit and humble heart at such a young age is one of the things that has inspired me. Thank you all for loving me when it's hard too and covering me in prayer. To all of my grandparents on earth and above, thank you for teaching me to dream big and think about my future. To all of my friends, thank you for your willingness to tell me your stories and the impacts you have each made in my life.

Contents

PART 3: Career

PART 1

Life

REAL LIFE STORIES – Tyra

Tyra devoted her time in high school to dance. When I say devoted I mean DEVOTED. Her schedule was wake up early, go to practice, school, homework, practice, and repeat. She never had time for friends or dating. Most girls at her high school were busy with getting guys to notice them, gossiping about who went to the house party Saturday night, and how drunk people got. When Tyra went to college, she quit dance. She developed confidence and had the time to make friends, go out, and talk to guys. Due to her lack of experience in high school, freshmen year, Tyra struggled with finding who she fit in with, and most of all, who she was as a woman. She began experimenting. She had her first drink, her first kiss, and many more firsts; to her surprise, her experiences led to heartbreak. When I interviewed Tyra, I asked her if she had the opportunity to talk to herself as a senior in high school, what she would share. She said, "Know who you are and what you want. Stick to your standards. Guys are so good at getting what they want. Most guys in college don't want anything serious, mostly sex or just a friend. You have to guard your heart. Have a schedule and get involved...it is the only way to survive."

Don't be naive. There are difficult times ahead. As the end approaches, people are going to be self-absorbed, money-hungry, self-promoting, stuck-up, profane, contemptuous of parents, crude, coarse, dog-eat-dog, unbending, slanderers, impulsively wild, savage, cynical, treacherous, ruthless, bloated windbags, addicted to lust, and allergic to God. They'll make a show of religion, but behind the scenes they're animals. Stay clear of these people. - 2 Timothy 3:1-5 (MSG)

Chapter 1
Your timer

The very moment you step on campus your timer starts. The seconds begin racing. The minutes keep rolling. Every hour becomes the most priceless thing to you. You start college as a fresh, high school graduate. You think you are ready, mature, and that you know it all. That was me at least. If this is you, you are in for a big awakening. The person you start college as is nothing like the person you are when you walk across that stage to receive your diploma for your undergraduate degree. College is about time. The word "time crunch" and "due date" will make you cringe. Naturally you adjust to your busy schedule. As a freshman, you'll think fourteen-credit-hours is unbearable, and when you reach midterms, it's the end of the world. You'll start to see that you have some free time. What do you do with it? You can sleep (that's always a favorite). You can eat (But you don't want to get the freshmen fifteen). You can build your social life by joining sororities, school clubs, or athletic teams. You can take up a new hobby or explore the city you are in. Staying busy is a major key to success in college. Living a well-scheduled lifestyle in college can prevent depression, being home sick, the common cold, social drama, bad grades, and even stupid choices. I'm not telling you to sign up for twenty hours, every school club, and play three sports. I'm simply encouraging you to live a well-rounded life. Staying busy and involved is not just to keep you sane in the craziness around you, but it's an easy way to reach the people around you and to be touched by the people ahead of you.

A big problem I had my first two years of college was finding the right kinds of friends and also finding the right version of me. I was so easily swayed, and my emotions were a jumbled mess. One day my mom lovingly explained that I was only nineteen. I don't know everything and at twenty-one I still don't! Getting involved with volunteer opportunities, finding out what I believe, and seeking new hobbies, led me to encounters with amazing people who I now consider my life long friends. I met girls that were older than me who "had been there and done that." Being teachable is so important, and it's not something that comes naturally.

Slow it down and take some time to work on you! Weirdly enough you can work on yourself by helping other people. Discover who you are and what you're made to do. God wants to use you, YES YOU, to do incredible things. It's your decision whether you're going just to sit in your room or get out there and find what your purpose is. You were not created to blend in with all the other faces, get your degree, and hopefully, find a guy to live happily ever after with. You are made to do extraordinary things. Whatever background you come from. Whoever your parents are. Whatever choices you have made. Today, it's about who you will become; what you do with your wisdom gained up until this point, determines that.

The verse above talks about the times of difficulty in our lives and has a description of people who may surround us. It seems very familiar... ungrateful, selfish, disobedient, without self-control. See the pattern? Girls, this is a description of the modern day female. We always want more. We choose our needs over others. We decide to do what feels natural, easy, and comfortable for us. We fall into a cycle of choices that slowly by surely can let us lose our self-control. We are afraid to go to the bathroom alone or eat at the lunch table by ourselves. We lack independence. We rely on guys and girls to make us feel worthy. Part of figuring out what God wants you to do with your life can simply begin with getting involved at your university or in your community. Be relational. It is so important to get to know different people and learn how to work and handle different personalities. Learning where other people come from can help you appreciate what you already have.

If you just so happen to cross paths with a girl who has an eating disorder, it's not an accident. If you meet a teen mom who shares her needs with you, it's not an accident. If you are introduced to a girl who has an addiction, an abusive relationship, or maybe just a girl who doesn't feel she's good enough; that is not an accident. Begin to realize from this moment forth, no encounter is an accident. Everyone you cross paths with has an affect on you just as much as you can affect them.

It's time for you to start evolving into a new woman. Say goodbye to the high school you. Are you ready?

So let me ask you a question, who are you? What's your story? What are your goals and plans for the future? I hope you have many questions answered by reading this book and that it will show you a glimpse of who you are meant to be.

Before we dive into the juicy content, here's a fun icebreaker. Take a look at the list below and put a check next to the tips you already use in your life. Grab a friend if you're currently with others and compare what your average day consists of. How do you do life?

Take a look at the 35 tips I have below that help me get all I can out of this beautiful life!

1. Start fresh every day
2. Check your bank statements
3. Don't hold grudges
4. Have a meatless Monday
5. Put away your phone when you're out to eat
6. Buy a planner
7. Cut back on sugar
8. Use a daily face moisturizer
9. Don't do drugs and if you do stop
10. Find a hobby
11. Exercise at least 3 days a week
12. Invest in good quality clothing

13. Read inspirational quotes or bible verses every morning
14. Don't skip your gyno appointment
15. Drink lots of agua
16. Drop loose change into a jar
17. Stand up for yourself
18. Remember to sleep!
19. Always wear a seatbelt
20. Take a day off
21. Make a beach trip at least once a year
22. Log out of your social media and give yourself a break
23. Learn to take constructive criticism
24. Stop letting the Internet diagnose you
25. Hugs solve everything
26. Don't take on everyone's problems
27. Spend time outside in the fresh air
28. Have a good relationship with your parents
29. Shop at thrift stores
30. Don't compare...yourself to others or past relationships to a present one.
31. Be aware that what you post on social media can affect your career
32. Indulge in random acts of kindness
33. 80% of people will like you 20% will not. That's ok!
34. Eat your vegetables
35. Let your face breathe without makeup for a day

Believe in yourself and understand that you are NOT going to understand everything that comes your way on your college journey. As you go through this guide, remember to be transparent with yourself in the journals. Everything happens for a reason, and you are here for a reason. You are reading this book for a reason! Don't waste your life and don't rush it away.

What are some ways you can use your free time to reach people around you?

What's holding you back?

How do you relate to Tyra?

#GGC with your thoughts for today
www.gabywrites.com

Journal

"What I'm trying to do here is to get you to relax, to not be so preoccupied with getting, so you can respond to God's giving. People who don't know God and the way he works fuss over these things, but you know both God and how he works. Steep your life in God-reality, God-initiative, God-provisions. Don't worry about missing out. You'll find all your everyday human concerns will be met." (Matthew 6: 31-33 MSG)

Chapter 2
The Buckets

We all come from different backgrounds and beliefs. Each of us has a dream or an image of ourselves that we wish we could be. We all have something that gives us pure happiness. In the story of the woman at the well in John 4, Jesus asks a Samaritan woman to draw Him some water from the well for a drink. He tells her about "living water" that God can give her where she will never thirst again. The woman replies with, "how can I get you water when you do not have a bucket?" Her focus was on the bucket. Like many of us, our focus isn't on the water but the bucket. We try different buckets throughout life. Buckets that get us more recognition, buckets that make us feel wanted, buckets that allow the pain to go away. The problem is, Jesus isn't concerned about the bucket. All He needs is you and your heart. You can't mix your buckets with the "living water". Honestly, you don't even need them. The amazing thing about this encounter is Jesus already knew the woman's heart. He knew about her baggage. He knew she had slept with a long list of men, had a few divorces, and the man she currently lived with wasn't even her husband. Jesus wants you to put down your bucket, give Him your baggage, and let Him have your heart.

In college, it's easy to get distracted and stray away. We go to church on Sundays and bring our already full buckets with us. They are full of our emotions, thoughts, and actions from the previous week. We share our buckets with God because that's what we have always been told to do right? Go to church on Sundays and always include Jesus! But Jesus doesn't want to share us with anyone or anything. He wants our whole hearts. He wants you to empty yourself of everything and let Him fill you up. Empty your bucket and let Him fill it with life.

Here are a few questions to help you diagnose how much of your heart you give to Jesus.

1) *How do you reward yourself throughout the week?*

After a hard week of classes and those long sleepless nights, the weekend cannot get here quick enough. To see where your heart honestly lies, you can just think about what you crave on a Thursday or Friday night. If you're a big people person, you're going to want to go out with a friend. Is it being held by your boyfriend? Buying yourself a new outfit? Spending countless hours creeping people on Instagram? Or maybe just going out to eat. Everyone has that one thing that makes the hard week worth it. The thing about giving your heart to Jesus is that He wants to be included in it all. Do your weekend plans reflect God in any way? Does your reward for the week come before your time spent with God? Could you give it up if He asked you to?

2) *What is the first thing you do when you're hurting from a breakup, failure, or loss?*

We have all been through a hurting moment. Breakups, death, failure, sickness; you can't get around it. So how do you deal with it? When you get bad news, who is the first person you call? For me, it's usually my mom. For others, it may be your best friend or boyfriend. Is that wrong? No. We were created to be relational; it's in our DNA. We are women. We CRAVE relationship. What makes it wrong is when we rely solely on the words and comfort from our friends and family more so then the promises and presence of Christ. It's almost like when a little girl trips and skins her knee. She's crying and searching for a familiar face on the playground. Her dad is sitting on a bench, and her friend is on the swings. She's obviously going to run to her daddy because he's the one that's always there for her. She knows he will fix her knee. She knows he will sacrifice his time and his money to make her feel better. She knows his love for her is deeper than anyone else's on that playground. It's not that her friend doesn't care or can't cheer her up. It's the fact that she knows her little friend doesn't have the power and ability to fix her knee. To make it stop bleeding or take her to the store and get a Band-Aid. This is God with our problems. Only He has the control and power to fix our skinned knees. Our friends and family can comfort us, but God can offer complete and total healing. Whether you handle circumstances with a substance, with spending money, secluding yourself, or even a friend, know it all cannot fully heal you inside.

3) *What are the qualities you wish you had or didn't have?*

Have you ever painted a picture or created something "artsy" you were proud of? Maybe you successfully made a Pinterest project that looks even better than the one you pinned. You decide you're going to give the painting to your best friend for her birthday because you're so proud of it. You watch as she unwraps the gift and looks at the painting you made for her. She smiles as to show your gesture was kind but then says, "Honestly, I wish you would have used more blue instead of red. And the way you painted the flower in this corner… it should have been made bigger. I just don't think I have much use for this anyways. You should have made it like the painting my other friend has. Her painting is much prettier." I can imagine your reaction wouldn't be too happy. Comparing ourselves to other people happens, and at times, it doesn't even faze us. When God created us, He put so much thought and effort into the blueprints. He took the time to design how you would look, how you would think, and how you would act. Your smile, skin tone, size, and personality was all His design. Think of how He feels every time we critique ourselves. It hurt Him deeply. Insecurity is not being selfless. When you hate on yourself, your focus is on YOURSELF. When our hearts are focused on all the flaws we think we have, our focus is not on what we can be doing for the gazillion other people on the planet. Living a selfless life is the ability to look past the lies your enemies feed you about your looks, your abilities, and your actions; it's about putting all of yourself aside to find ways to build other women up around you. It's called God-Confidence.

Challenge:

What are the things you hate about yourself? Do you know of someone who has similar insecurities? How can you help a girl in your life to grow some God-Confidence? What is inside your bucket? Who or what has your heart?

Share your thoughts #GGC
www.gabywrites.com

Journal

Chapter 3
Made from bone

The very first love story is found in the very first book of the Bible. When God made Eve, He put His all into her to show off His glory. Eve was not Adam's idea. This creation was a love story made by God. God was technically the founder of Match.com and created a match made in heaven: "It's not good for the Man to be alone; I'll make him a helper, a companion." (Gen. 2:18-24) (MSG). Eve was God's idea.

Yes, Women were made to be a help to the man, but we have slightly missed the point. We weren't made to be controlled by a man and do everything in our power to please a guy or get them to notice us. Eve was God's idea, made for God's glory. In your daily life, this is something to remember. You reflect who God is. Every ounce of who you are and every detail of your image is from God. Knowing this, we should hold our heads high and present ourselves as the masterpieces we were intended to be. Yes we are meant to encourage our significant other but we are more so meant to live life abundantly. Let people be so in awe of the way you live, your attitude, and actions; let other women desire the joy you have.

"Whatever the man called the animals, that was their name. There were male and female animals.

But for Adam, there was not another like him or fit for him. God put the Man into a deep sleep. As he slept, he removed one of his ribs and replaced it with flesh. God then used the rib that he had taken from the Man to make Woman and presented her to the Man." (21-22 MSG)

Why did God wait to create Eve? He created the animals and allowed Adam to name them all. Adam had it made. He had a giant man cave called earth and unlimited food. I believe God waited so He could show Adam that just like the animals had another like them, Adam was not meant to be alone either.

Why were they made on different days?

By creating Adam and Eve on different days, God was purposely saving His best for last. He was drawing Adam's attention to the gift of Eve. She was special and made to not only help him and be by his side, but to lead the generations of women to come. God saved the best beauty and final creation for last.

I heard a story from a Pastor's wife about how she visited a tribe in Africa and met a woman there. The woman had stayed by her husband's side through everything; even in his old age when he could no longer walk or move from place to place. She dressed him, fed him, and cared for him. I'm not telling you this to say we are meant to clean, cook, and be slaves. Oh no. The treasure is this: when the pastor's wife asked her how she did it, the African woman replied, "Man was made from dust and dirt. Woman was made from bone. You put dirt in boiling water, it disappears. You put bone in boiling water, it is still bone and still strong." God created women to be strong. Next time you feel as if you are put into a pot of boiling water, remember you won't whither away. You were made from bone and formed from the hands of a perfect Creator. You were His final and most treasured creation. You are a gift to the world.

Challenge:

What is your view of yourself?

What do others think of you?

Do you feel you need friends or a guy in your life to give you confidence and strength?

Are you comfortable spending time on your own?

Share your thoughts #GGC
gabywrites.com

Journal

Chapter 4
The Freshmen 15

When I started college, I was not worried about gaining weight or losing weight. I was perfectly happy with my size. I was an athlete in high school (not a very good one) but I still got my exercise in every week. After high school, I never had any exercise. I started going out to eat late at night to Cookout and Waffle House with my friends. I would choose to eat whatever I wanted, and this was a literal reflection of my current life choices. I was choosing to do whatever I wanted and not necessarily what was best for me. I had no idea why I began gaining weight so rapidly. I didn't notice the weight until my clothes began to fit tighter and my dad so lovingly told me I had gained some weight since he last saw me. I wasn't happy with my weight and at the same time, I wasn't happy with my life. After seeing a doctor in Myrtle Beach, I was diagnosed with a hormonal disorder called PCOS, and he advised me to change some habits in my life. He said to stay away from:

- Sugar
- Carbohydrates
- White flour
- Dairy

Besides the diet, he told me to do at least 30 minutes of cardio five to six days a week. I honestly didn't take his advice seriously and just kept gaining weight until I came back from a trip to Spain. I saw a picture of myself and my heart sank. "That isn't me", I thought. I looked very bloated all over, and my smile looked forced. I knew I was unhappy. From April of 2015 until August 1st of 2015, I worked as hard as I could and lost a whopping 25lbs! By following the diet advice he gave me and doing at least 30 minutes of cardio six days a week, the pounds began to melt off my body. This made me think how often God gives us a way out. He gives us a way to lose hurt from our lives.

If we struggle with depression, He says, "God's a safe-house for the battered, a sanctuary during bad times. The moment you arrive, you relax; you're never sorry you knocked." (Psalms 9:9-10 MSG)

If you struggle with a heavy heart He says, "Worry weighs us down; a cheerful word picks us up." (Proverbs 12:25 MSG)

If you're struggling with fear He says," Be strong. Take courage. You will enter the land with this person, this land that God promised their ancestors that he'd give them. You will make them the proud possessors of it. God is striding ahead of you. He's right there with you. He won't let you down; he won't leave you. Don't be intimidated. Don't worry."- (Deuteronomy 31:8 MSG)

If you're going through a hard time, "For I the LORD thy God will hold thy right hand, saying unto thee, Fear not; I will help thee." (Isaiah 41:13 MSG)

If you need peace, He says, "That's right. Because I, your God, have a firm grip on you, and I'm not letting go. I'm telling you, 'Don't panic. I'm right here to help you.' (John 14:27MSG)

If you are seeking God with a need in your life, He says, "You can be sure that God will take care of everything you need, his generosity exceeding even yours in the glory that pours from Jesus. (Philippians 4:19 MSG)

If you are struggling with guilt He says,
"We admit our sins—make a clean breast of them—he won't let us down; He'll be true to Himself. He'll forgive our sins and purge us of all wrongdoing. (1 John 1:9 MSG)

The point is there's a correlation between discipline for your body and your soul. Claiming God's promises and listening to His instructions on how to get through every day successfully, is just as important as taking care of your body every day. Working out and following my diet plan not only made me lose weight, but it gave me confidence, relieved stress, cleared up acne, and changed my mood. Choosing to workout is the hardest thing about working out and that's just like making time everyday to talk to God. When I started having a quiet time to reflect on my day, release my emotions, and reconnect with God, I began to see my life in a whole new way. I realized I was making some not so great choices in my life, and I'm not talking about eating. After losing my mema and papa to cancer my freshmen and sophomore year, I started to rely on other people and things to make me happy again. It was easier to hide my hurt and cover it up then it was to come face to face with it. I started to hate church. I didn't want to leave my room and at times when I left my room, it was with people who could care less about me. In the middle of all of this, me and my boyfriend of almost three years broke up. I started to want attention from guys. I wanted a ton of friends at college, and I wanted to just make the craziest memories. It's normal to crave relationships. That's in our God-given DNA. It's not okay to put those relationships over God. It's not okay to depend on how many guys think you're hot or how many girls think you're a great friend. On the other hand, it's also not okay to live your life in a way where you only follow a list of rules so people think you're the world's godliest woman. I was craving the wrong things in my diet and my life. I realized three things:

I needed to exercise.
(So I did five to six times a week)

I needed to count my blessings.
(So I wrote down three things I was thankful for everyday)

I needed to surround myself with women who were real about life and who encouraged me to be the best version of myself. *(So I joined a women's bible study through my church and volunteered in the care/counseling department in the youth group)*

I challenge you after reading this chapter to create a plan to stay active physically and mentally while at college. Write out a plan you can do every week to create a healthy body and soul.

You don't have to do it alone either. Go to the school gym with your friend or do a Zumba video with your roommate to dance off the fat. Make a plan for your spiritual life. Spend some time alone reading a few verses when you wake up or maybe during lunch. Thank God for something while you shower. Every day may have a different amount of free time based on your classes, so mentally decide when you can devote some time to give to God. Pray continually and claim a different promise each day for whatever you are needing.

Challenge

Do you have an exercise plan?

Do you have a set time you spend time with God?

What promise above do you need to claim?

Share your thoughts #GGC

For free printable exercise plans visit www.gabywrites.com

Journal

Independent Thoughts:

To prepare for the Guys Section coming up, read 2 Samuel 13 and 1Corinthians 13:4-8

How does the story of Amnon show you the difference between lust and love?

Write down the definitions of Love and Lust.

Based on 1 Corinthians 13:4-8 what are the characteristics of Love?

Are you living a life of lust or love with your friendships, relationship, and with God?

Do you just like the benefits God gives you but give nothing in return? Are you impatient with unanswered prayers? Is a guy rushing you into a relationship you aren't ready for? Do you put others needs over your own?

PART 2

Guy

REAL LIFE STORIES- Samantha

Samantha has always been independent. She's had no choice. Seeing how she grew up without a dad in her life, her only example at home has been her mom. When she was just fifteen, she worked to help pay her mom's bills. Sam is stunning and quite outgoing. As she got older, attention from older guys caused her to eventually lose something special and begin a cycle of hurt. This only brought confusion. She never really had an example of what a good guy was like, and this caused indecisiveness with what kind of man she wanted. To this day, Sam still sometimes endures the struggles with commitment due to fear of getting used or hurt. At times, she feels nothing and second-guesses everything in her career choices, friendships, and dating relationships. There were times in college where Sam did not know what kind of guy she wanted or if she wanted a relationship at all. As soon as she ended one, she felt as though she has to get into another, to feel secure. It creates anxiety for her. When I asked Sam what advice she would give her younger self about guys, she said, "Guys .....They are so good at telling you what you want to hear. I can trust way too easily. My ideal guy would be someone I can go on random adventures with. Someone who will always make me laugh. Someone who will take care of me as much as I care for them and someone who is straight up with what they want."

"I know what I'm doing. I have it all planned out—plans to take care of you, not abandon you, plans to give you the future you hope for." (jeremiah 29:11 MSG)

Chapter 5
God values women

If you've ever read the bible, you can agree with me that certain books are not easy to read, especially the ones with genealogies. Bazaar son of "name I can't pronounce", Judah son of "another name I can't pronounce"... it's just not fun. Never ending lists of different men's names and where they come from. In Matthew chapter 1, the author gives us the list of Jesus' ancestors. The list begins with men like Abraham and Isaac but then something unseen happens. Women are mentioned, and not just any women. Women who were considered to be sinful in their times. Ones carrying a lot of baggage.

First, we have Tamar, who had sex with her father-in-law (Judah) and got pregnant. After she is shunned and left with nothing, Judah tries to be a double standard and have her stoned. Eventually, he says in Genesis 38 that she is more worthy than he was and helped her provide a life for the child.

Rahab is next. She was a prostitute and a Gentile, living in Jericho (Josh. 2:1). Despite her occupation, she was selfless and provided financially for her parents and siblings. We also know her as the one willing to hide the Israelite spies who have come to search out a way to attack and defeat Jericho.

The third is Ruth, who is also a Gentile, but her story was a little different. Most know that Ruth and her sister-in-law lost their husbands. When their mother in law tells them to go back home and find new men, Ruth decides to stay and live with her widowed mother-in-law to care and provide. In fact, After she finds Boaz he identifies her as a woman of virtue, a woman of noble character (Ruth 3:11).

The fourth woman is Uriah's wife. Yup, the one who was bathing on the roof while her husband was at war. She was seduced by King David and becomes pregnant with his child. We all know what happened next. David has General Uriah placed in the front of the battle where he is sure to be killed.

The last woman mentioned is Mary, who was the wife of Joseph. Luke 1:35-38 shows her character when the angel tells her she's going to become pregnant with the Son of God. Imagine her thoughts; she would have to convince her husband, family, and community, that Jesus was placed inside of her by the Holy Spirit and not from doing the dirty with another man. This stuff didn't happen every day. Imagine if that was you trying to tell your boyfriend you haven't been cheating! Or trying to tell your parents you never had sex before but you were pregnant? Tough one.

The reason I'm telling you all of this is to say that all of the women He included in His genealogy were misfits, unknown, baggage carriers, unwanted, and poor. They all had hurt in their lives but through Christ were used to do amazing things. A genealogy is to show who you have come from. Jesus says He came from a line of WOMEN, who were sinners, and He left this world by giving His life to save sinners like me and you. How amazing is it that a perfectly, holy God would associate with women; women that were far from perfect.

Knowing how valued you are to Christ, make sure you value yourself highly as well. Set your standards for finding a guy that will treat you like a princess and that wants to do nothing but let you blossom into the woman you were made to be.

Challenge:

Write out a list of women in your family. Think of where you come from and where you are going!

In what ways are you different from women fifty years ago?

Why do you think many people from the millennial age down Generation Y?

How can you begin to change how others view women your age?

Share your thoughts #GGC
www.gabywrites.com

Journal

Chapter 6
Guys Talk

In Part 2 of the book, I interviewed several college guys to answer all of the many questions we have in our heads but never know who to ask. You can thank me later. Warning.... some of these answers you won't want to hear while others are a surprise. The guys interviewed all come from different backgrounds and beliefs. Dating in college is completely different than high school. For me, my dad was not the most lenient with me dating before college, but that doesn't mean I didn't push the limits and have a boyfriend. Of course, he was always right about the guys I brought home and all my high school relationships never worked out. Going away to college, my mom and dad weren't there to tell me who I could or couldn't go out with. In college, enjoy the fun of meeting new guys and going on dates. Understand that the big difference is that it's all up to you. Your parents aren't there to put in their two-cents. You have to know who you are as a woman and who you need in your life. This is what you may experience whether you attend a public or private university. Before we get into the topic of "guys", I thought I would cover an important pre-requisite.

Choosing for yourself

A big mistake many girls make before they start their freshmen year is allowing their future decisions to be based on what their boyfriend encourages them to do. There is nothing wrong with sharing your concerns with your boyfriend about deciding on a college, choosing a major, and joining if you should join a sorority. The problem comes into play when you allow your guy, especially your 18-year-old boyfriend, to dictate where you go or what you major in. Some key facts to remember are this:

Your relationship status can change

No matter what you say, take it from someone who's been there, you don't know what can happen. I was in a three-year relationship with a guy, and I was for certain that I was going to marry him while I taught 3rd graders somewhere in Myrtle Beach, SC. Here's the reality: We broke up my freshmen year. I changed my major to Broadcast Media, I'm now with an entirely different guy, and I've decided to live in the Upstate of South Carolina. Go figure. You have to realize that in college you evolve into a completely different woman. You go from high school girl to career woman in four years.

You can change

As I said before, I had my life planned out on Pinterest. I thought I knew every detail and how it would happen. The funny thing is, I am so glad God is the one writing my story and not me. I love my life way better now than how I was planning it to be. Going away to college taught me some things: independence, responsibility, and financial maturity. I realize it's not about your social life. It's okay not to have a ton of friends. Something my best friend posted says this amazingly; "I'd rather have a 401K than 401K followers." I've realized it's crucial to start saving money now and not spend it all on new clothes and weekend outings. I've also realized outside of college, there is a whole other pool of fish. Some of these fish are real men with real ambitions, responsibilities, and maturity. Don't think you have to start college with a boyfriend or that you have to graduate college with a ring by spring. Just get your degree and let God do the rest. You have your whole life to be married to someone! Work on yourself.

Positive in and negative out

Guys who can't take your future seriously shouldn't be taken seriously. Friends who constantly degrade you and try to convince you that you're too young to be taking your life seriously; you need to get rid of them. Surround yourself with people who want you to succeed in all areas of life. As women, we are so bad with this. Jealousy quickly takes over in situations where we feel threatened. A beautiful girl gets engaged to a successful and attractive guy, she snags an incredible job, and she has no financial worries. Another girl is wishing for a guy to give her attention, dreading her next day at work (because it's a job she settled for), and hoping she can afford the next loan payment. This is life. Life is what you make it and sometimes our lives map out differently than others. I challenge you to surround yourself with positive women who don't sit and talk about other women negatively. They don't degrade you, they have good energy, and they don't throw their time in college away on partying and getting the attention of every guy on the sport's teams. Focus on getting the right kind of attention from the CEO at your dream job. Impress your parents. Make a difference in the community. Spend time with your grandparents. Do thoughtful things for your friends. Find a church that feeds you every Sunday. Find God for yourself. Let Him write your love story.

With all of this in mind, think about the following questions before moving on to the "guy" section.

Do you feel that your relationship is hindering you?

Do your friends encourage you to be your best?

How do you make your important choices? Who do you turn to for advice?

Question and answer

Question:

Is it true guys in college only want a hookup?

Guy's Answer:

If you are willing to give us what we want then yes some of us will take it. It depends on who the guy is and what he feels is wrong. Not all guys are jerks. Some of us are ready for a girlfriend and others just don't want that commitment. For me, I'm only twenty years old. I'm focused on playing lacrosse and graduating. If the right girl comes along, then that can change.

Question:

"Is it weird if a girl wants to wait until she's married to have sex?"

Guy's Answer:

"I respect that. It's hard to find now a days, but It doesn't make or break a relationship for me. I mean if you have slept with fifty guys then I'm going to rethink it, but people change, I'm not going to judge a girl on whether she is a virgin or not. There are way more important qualities. If she's that amazing and a guy really wants her then he can wait as hard as that is."

Question:

"Why can't I get a guy to commit?"

Guy's Answer:

"I'd really have to know you and the guy, but it could be a lot of things. He could have had his heart broken, and he's scared. He could have never had a serious relationship, so he doesn't know how. He could be really focused on his career or sports he plays. It could even be there's an issue with you... maybe your attitude or something you do?"

Question: Do guys want to date their freshmen year?

Guy's Answer:

"Unless we come in with a relationship, we are just trying to feel out the waters. My freshmen year I was scoping out to see who is available, who is dating material, and who just wants to be friends with benefits. Girls change a lot in college but freshmen year is when everyone is still fresh out of high school."

Questions: Why is it considered trashy when girls have slept around but it's something to be congratulated when guys get with the whole population?

Guy's Answer: "Different guys want different things. If they just want a hookup, then they are going to get with the easiest girl possible and then brag about it. It's not us guys that usually talk bad about the girls who sleep around. Yeah, we joke and make remarks about her, but it's usually their own friends or other females at school who hate. Girls are hateful."

Question: Will guys not date me because I've gotten "Around"?

Guy's Answer: "After I had become a Christian my junior year in college, I met a girl that had sex with a good amount of people. I couldn't judge because I had done the same thing but it did kill me that she was so easily swayed by guys that were only out for sex. She's so beautiful in every way, and I like that I found someone who loves me for me. Every guy is different and every situation is different. Never settle for someone who will make you feel guilty for your past choices. Find someone who looks past your past"

My relationship:

I met my man through my best friend and her ex-boyfriend. At the time, I did not want to be in a committed relationship with anyone. I agreed to meet him and it just so happens I met him on his 21st birthday. It wasn't love at first sight. I didn't know I was going to marry him or that he was "the one" from that first night. By the second week of us talking, I realized I *wanted* him to be the one. I had never dated a guy that looked like him or acted like him. I liked it. He made such an effort to catch my attention and still everyday, he makes me know how much he loves me. The first place he took me was his church. Little did he know by inviting me to his church, my brother, my parents, and me would be radically changed. I've NEVER been in a relationship like this. We don't discuss every little detail about our past relationships and choices nor do we care too. I've never wanted to spend so much time with one person. I could look into his sweet blue eyes every day. I love the way his rough calloused hands feel because I know he is a hard worker. Being a foot taller than me, I automatically feel protected. He is so selfless and puts me before himself. He admits when he's wrong and tells me when I'm right. We don't fight or make a big deal out of silly things. We don't have similar hobbies, occupations, or history. He likes golf and I like working out. He's a welder and I'm in the Media industry. He was born and raised in the south and I was born and raised in the north. Our differences allow us to compliment each other while our similar beliefs and feelings allow us to connect on a deeper level. He meets my needs and I meet his. He communicates things equally as much as I do. He shows me he cares as much as I show him I care. He loves church and that is so hard to find in a guy his age. He loves to laugh and try new things just like me. I had it all wrong and it took me the summer before my senior year of college to see it. God wrote my story. I wasted so much time trying to find a guy in high school and all through college but there was no way I could find him in the places I was looking. It doesn't matter how hard you look for a guy, how many parties and events you attend, or how many people you match with on Tinder. You can't write your love story. God already wrote it. He used my roommate to let His plans unfold and he will use someone to do the same for you.

Challenge

What questions and answers shocked you most?

What questions do you have for guys?

Share your thoughts #GGC
www.gabywrites.com

Journal

Chapter 7
The Ideal Woman (according to them)

Almost every woman has had the same questions when it comes to men. I took it upon myself to interview EIGHT men in their twenties through a series of similar questions. They come from many different backgrounds and beliefs. I did this because in college there's a vast sea of guys. They all come from different places and were raised in different views. It's important to know your worth as a woman and know what you desire in a guy. So what does a guy want in a girl? Surprisingly they all had a few similar answers on what they want in a girlfriend/wife. Here it is in an easy 10-item list:

10. INDEPENDENCE

One of the biggest relationship issues caused by women is being too clingy with our men. When I asked one guy what his biggest turn off was, he replied with one word, "NEEDINESS". Now don't get me wrong, guys love spending quality time with their significant other. The issue comes along when we as women have to text all day long or be with our boyfriend all day every day to feel this sense of affirmation. Men love a girl who has her own life, her own means of making money, her own group of friends, and a sense of independence. Don't make the mistake of kicking your friends and life to the curb over a boy. He is NOT worth that. Make him a priority but give him SPACE! A little space will allow him to think about you, even more, when you're not around. If you feel as though you don't have anything else to do except visit him here's some help: Volunteer, grab coffee with your friends, hit the gym, or spend time with your parents.

9. CONVERSATION

Ephesians 4:29 says, "Watch the way you talk. Let nothing foul or dirty come out of your mouth. Say only what helps, each word a gift." (MSG)

Many times as women we all can admit we get caught up in gossip or always making the conversation about ourselves. To find a guy who you can vent to and he will actually listen; this is a priceless thing. Do not confuse gossiping about your friends lives with venting about your life. Guys do not want to hear about all the bad choices your friends are making and honestly how is that bettering either of you? Be sure to show concern about his life and not always make it about you and your issues. Choose your words wisely and always create a positive environment for the both of you! One guy mentioned in the interview, "When she always talks about herself or her friends and never asks about me I feel invisible. I want someone to encourage me and create a positive atmosphere."

8. APPEARANCE

We obsess as women over beauty secrets and finding new ways to become the most wanted female around. We try different makeup and hair colors. Craving to be noticed, we wear the sexiest dress we can find when we go out. One of the Guys told me in the interview that although appearance is important, "The most physically attractive women to me are the ones who have a good attitude, beautiful smile, and make an effort to stay in shape." In shape is not only with eating healthy and staying active, but just taking care of yourself as a woman through good hygiene and finding ways to make your life less stressful.

7. ATTITUDE

Proverbs 15:1 says, "A gentle response defuses anger, but a sharp tongue kindles a temper-fire." (MSG)

I was out to dinner with my boyfriend a few weeks ago, and we sat near a couple that had my attention. The boyfriend was simply asking the girl some questions, and she was giving him the biggest attitude back and degrading him in the process. Now I do not know the entire situation but from my interviews with these guys I can tell you a bad attitude pushes them far away. They want a girlfriend who brings peace and positivity to their lives. College, our jobs, and people can so easily stress us out. If you have a stressful life, use i\t as a way to bring God glory. When people see how much you can smile through it all, they will be dying to know your secret! And simply, it's Jesus. Realize that you can control the mood and outcome of your day by just choosing encouraging words or negative ones. This statement leads us to our next point.

6. TRUST

Oh boy. This word pokes some of you the wrong way. We've all had our trust broken whether it was by a family member, friend, or a guy. Dating in college is so different than high school. You are dating with the intentions of spending the rest of your life with someone…or at least you should be. The most common thing I hear nowadays in relationships is, "I have trust issues" or "I was hurt so many times I can't trust anybody." Sadly if this is you, I'm sorry. I've been hurt too. I'm also guilty of hurting other people. We are human, and life goes on. Don't swim around in your sorrows and expect your new boyfriend to swim around with you. Start fresh and trust him. If you claim you have been hurt so many times then what do you have to lose? Going on a deeper level, do not allow yourself to be hurt knowing someone is not right for you. If you choose to date someone who wants sex or is a big party animal and that is not you, you're setting yourself up for hurt. Do not be a missionary dater, Just don't. Bad idea.

5. PERSONALITY:

This one is big. This word was one key thing mentioned in every guy's interview because personality can make or break a relationship. Some key factors that play into a real personality are based on what a particular guy wants. One thing the guys in my interview kept mentioning is that they want a positive and transparent girl who isn't afraid to get their hands dirty or break a sweat.

4. Confidence

You have heard this over and over again. Confidence is sexy. I'm not saying to walk around in your panties at Wal-Mart because you're confident you look good. I'm saying not to seek the approval of others, especially your man, to make you feel good about yourself. If you need your boyfriend to tell you that you look pretty every single day, I must regretfully inform you that it won't last for long. A Guy notices when the girl he's talking to posts a ton of selfies and does things for attention. They are getting smarter ladies. Find confidence in helping others, establishing a successful career, exercising, or taking up a new hobby. Put your phone away for a change and take a break from the social media. Find your happy place.

3. ACTIVE:

As Matthew 6:31-33 says, "What I'm trying to do here is to get you to relax, not to be so preoccupied with getting, so you can respond to God's giving. People who don't know God and the way he works fuss over these things, but you know both God and how he works. Steep your life in God-reality, God-initiative, God-provisions. Don't worry about missing out. You'll find all your everyday human concerns will be met."

The word active reminds me of the days when I used Instant Messaging, and I had to change my status to offline or active. Although every guy I interviewed wanted a girl who is in shape, I'm not only talking about active as in exercise but in what you do with your time. Don't be afraid to take risks and try new things. Go kayaking, hiking, or lay under the stars together. If you hate football, but he loves it, Sit with him during his game. Just be there for him and be active in his life. Nothing will allow you both to grow closer together then when you are seeking God and actively doing things to help others meet God. Men know when mentally you are "offline" and unsupportive. Get active!

2. Let HIM wear the pants

I mean there's not much I can say about this one. It's self-explanatory. Let your man be the man and wear the pants. I'm not saying to date a control freak no one likes that. I'm also not saying to let your guy lead you in the wrong direction.

Guys want to feel like a man and that they are taking care of you. Don't take their role away from them. I mean, it's God-given One guy in my interview stated, " When a woman has to control everything and make all the decisions in our relationship, I start to shut down."

1. Make him want to be a better man

Whatever you do and whatever happens in your life, people will come and go. It's important that we don't lose sight of what is important, and that is being an encouragement to others around us. Spread love and peace. I'm not trying to go all earth hippie on you, but it's the truth. Sadly, you may not marry the guy you're currently dating. Maybe after reading this list you might think, "Hey, maybe I'm not compatible with Freddy." Whatever happens, make sure you have both gained something positive out of the experience. Make him want to be a better man. I love what my dad says about my mom and her attitude. He tells me all the time that due to her positive spirit and giving heart, after a fight or him raising his voice, he immediately has to apologize because she just makes him want to be the best husband he can be and treat her like a queen. I love it! Grow together spiritually or if you are reading this and you are not into the "God thing"… just build each other up.

Challenge:

What numbers do you feel are your strengths?

Have you noticed a lack of any of these in a current or past relationship?

Make a list of 10 traits you want in a guy and compare them to this list.

Share your thoughts #GGC
www.gabywrites.com

Journal

Independent thoughts:

To prepare for the career section read Acts 16:9-40.

What was Lydia's Career?

How did God use her talent and career path to impact the world?

PART 3
Career

REAL LIFE STORIES- MANDY

Mandy has two homes. One from her birth mom and the other with her adopted family. She still keeps in contact with her birth mom, but there's something inspirational about her family. Knowing they chose to care for her and love her no matter where she came from; They encouraged her to follow her dreams. Mandy loves to run, and cross-country is her thing. When she didn't have the best day, she would run and run for miles until endorphins would mellow the negativity. Many people never realized the past she had come from because her beautiful smile and sweet laughter always made it seem like everything was okay. Mandy chose to go to college and run cross-country but knew the struggle that comes with being adopted; she passionately majors in criminal justice. Mandy is planning on going to law school so she can be a child advocate in the courtroom. She found a passion and ran with it. When I asked Mandy what she would tell girls about college Mandy said, " Just stay focused and find what makes you happy. Always make God first. Surround yourself with friends that are going to bring you up and distance yourself from the girls that create negative in your life. Distancing myself from negative people was the best choice I made and helped me fix the reputation I got from stupid choices I made with them."

"If God gives such attention to the appearance of wildflowers—most of which are never even seen—don't you think He'll attend to you, take pride in you, do His best for you?" (Matthew 6:30 MSG)

Chapter 8
Spiritual Stretch Marks

There's one thing all women hate about their appearance, and we can all relate: stretch marks. Did you just cringe? I did. Why must we get stretch marks! It's just not fair. Women have tried different things to fade the marks like lotion, exercise, and the tanning bed. Some people even use Crisco. Yes, people actually slab that gunky stuff on their skin and yes that's the stuff used to make fried chicken. We all relate to the stretch marks on our bodies but have you noticed any spiritual stretch marks? This might sound odd to you, and it did to me too. I was mentored in high school by my Pastor's wife. She would share with me stories off how she got different spiritual stretch marks, and I started to catch on to how and why she got them and that I actually had them too!

How do you know if you have them? Let's take a look at some famous women in the Bible. Pick anyone. We can start with Esther. She lived with her Uncle Mordecai because her parents were killed. Fast forward to when she was chosen to be queen after a long process and she was faced with the scary task of coming to the King's court without an invite to talk about her people. She struggled with this task that her uncle asked her to do. She was obviously chosen to do it by God if we look at the bigger picture. So what made her struggle? Fear, worry, insecurities. What caused these insecurities? There's not much about her life in the Bible, but we know her parents were killed and then she was taken from her only guardian to be put in a giant beauty pageant. After all she had been through, it's safe to say Esther had some spiritual stretch marks. She was growing and stretching due to her traumatic experiences that she could not control.

Because God saw her growth, He knew she could easily take on the task as long as she did not focus on herself and kept her eyes on Him. See spiritual stretch marks are a good thing unlike the ones on our body. Because we are so used to hating the physical marks, we start to critique the stretch marks on our heart. Maybe you have:

- lost a family member or friend
- been broken up with
- failed
- been cheated on
- physical abuse
- been emotionally abused
- lied to
- lonely
- in a dark place
- sexually harassed

- in debt
- made a choice you regret

All of these hurts cause spiritual stretch marks as we get through them, and God notices that. He wants to use your stretch marks to tell a story and bring Him glory. If we wallow in our hurt and pasts mistakes, He can't use us. If we take the focus off of our own insecurities and regrets, we can begin to be transparent with other females around us who may have been hurt in the same way. You never know how God will use you. So how does this connect to a career?

God may have a particular career path He wants you to take. Until you get over yourself and look into new avenues, He may not be able to show you what He wants you to do. Get creative and see how you can blossom into that confident woman you're meant to be.

Challenge:

Do you have any spiritual stretch marks?

What caused them?

How can you begin to take the focus off of yourself and become transparent with your heart?

How has God used your stretch marks to shape you today?

Share your thoughts #GGC
www.gabywrites.com

Journal

Chapter 9
Money Maker

Let's be real…college is not cheap. If you aren't smart enough to get a full ride based on academic achievement, you're excluded from most of the scholarships given by your university. In my personal experience, I came out of high school with a 3.8 GPA, but my SAT score was barely 900. Freshmen year I was awarded academic scholarships based on the GPA I brought in, but slowly I began to lose them when my GPA went down to a 3.2. I then started searching for ways to get scholarship money online and here are a few sites that have been helpful:

- FASFA
- College Board
- Fun Aid
- Upromise
- Savingforcollege.com
- Fast Web
- Sallie Mae

Unfortunately, the reality is most of us will have student loans to pay off when we graduate. I know I do. Writing this as a senior in college, I am already stressing out over the image of the debt piling up before my eyes. Everyone gets through it. So I Know you will too. Don't stress out over paying for college.

- Speak to the business office and explain your situation
- Look for random scholarships online
- Work the summer before you start school and put away money

Did you know:

Six months after you graduate you are required to start paying back your loans. How can you start making money now without a degree?

Earn cash without a boss

Being an entrepreneur comes naturally to me. My parents never went to college, and that is because my dad had a keen eye for business opportunity and worked hard. Nowadays a degree is required for just about everything. Having a job your freshmen year is not the smartest idea, but it's possible. Depending on where your university is located, you could have to drive a far distance and waste gas. Homework and tests are unpredictable at times so you may get scheduled to work on a day you should have your face in the book. I'm all about a working but what if working in college is difficult for the place where you are in your life? I have a few solutions that have brought success to my bank account.

Start an online small business:

If you're a crafty person, start a business selling things on Etsy, Amazon, or Ebay. I would buy old 80's jeans from Goodwill for $3.99 and turn them into super cute high-waist jeans. They sell like hot cakes. Just sit down and think of something cute and inexpensive for you to create!

Here are some ideas:

- o Crochet or T-shirt scarves
- o Glamorous Dog Collars
- o Band Tshirts
- o Custom beach coolers
- o Headbands
- o Jewelry
- o Body Scrub
- o Witty Mug

Sell your unwanted clothes to consignment shops
(Plato's Closet, Clothes Mentor, local consignment)

The key to selling to used clothing stores is quality and demand. Don't try to sell your shorts in the winter and expect them to buy them. They won't. Also, don't expect a used clothing store to buy anything stained, ripped, or stinky. They are paying you cash for your items so expect them to be slightly picky. Don't be afraid to ask around and see if any of your friends have clothes they don't want!

Get Paid to take polls, grade websites, use search engines, and test out new products.

Sometimes these can be scams, but there are some authentic companies out there. A few I've successfully tried are:

- o   Pinecone Research
- o   User testing
- o   Swagbucks

* The best-paying ones always have a long application process but you get up to $10 per survey you take and it goes through PayPal, or you can have them send a check*

Get Paid to Tutor

If you're not the crafty type but math and science are your forte then I'd advise you to use that to your advantage! Talk to teachers and find out if anyone needs help in certain areas.

Sell and market a product to your campus

Most colleges have are fraternities, sororities, and student organizations. They all have matching shirts, cups, coasters, bags, sunglasses, ect. This is a forever growing market that you should take advantage pf. Keep up with the latest styles and see what you can create and market to these student groups. You could create hand-painted custom coolers that have a monogram or Greek letters on the top. By purchasing iron on printer paper and t-shirts from Wal-Mart, you can have your own t-shirt business; creating shirts for these organizations. The possibilities are endless and Pinterest is a wonderful brain-storming tool to use for this.

Get paid to advertise on your blog or YouTube.

If you are familiar with Google Analytics, this is nothing new to you. By increasing your followers and viewers, Google notices and will pay you for allowing ads on your blog or YouTube. For every ad that is clicked, you receive money. It's as easy at that. You just need your own domain and a large follower basis.

Lastly, Just be smart with your money.

Being raised in church every Sunday, I heard sermon after sermon about being smart with your money and giving back to God. In my personal experience, whenever I'm most thankful for what I have already and when I am freely giving back to God, that is when I seem to become more and more successful. Get involved in community service and volunteer somewhere. You'll be surprised the doors that open up and the reward you receive that's way greater than any whopping amount of money you could get. My first internship in college, I'll never forget the words my director said.

College is not about the grades you make but the hands that you shake! Not saying to fail your classes but hands-on experiences and relationships made are what get you those life changing opportunities.

Challenge:

Have you figured out how you are paying for college?

What are some ways you can make money during college?

What are some places you can volunteer for that have something to do with your major?

List some ideas you have!

#GGC with your thoughts for today

Visit www.gabywrites.com for a free printable budget, savings plan sheet, and longer list of money-making ideas.

Journal

Chapter 10
Marketing Yourself

Until my senior year, I did not see the importance of starting to market myself early on. After talking with professors and going to different seminars, I realized that your career path begins the moment you start your first day of college. You make your career happen. Your teachers don't make it happen, and neither do your parents. It's all you. What are some ways to get noticed by the companies you wish to work for?

1) A phenomenal resume.

Obviously being a college student you don't have much experience. This is why I cannot stress enough the importance of volunteering and interning while you're in college. Your resume when you graduate should only be a page, but what you put on that page can make the biggest impression. You can visit your school's career resource center to learn more about building a resume.

2) An online portfolio

Do not throw away your projects and work. I repeat. DO NOT. Save all of your work on a flash drive and upload the work onto an online portfolio. I use wix.com. You can choose a free website or pay for a domain for a monthly fee. For example, I am a broadcast media major. I have an about me page, my resume, my projects (videos I've made, PR campaigns, etc), an article page (for my writing skills), and a contact page. I also link my social media at the bottom so they can go ahead and view it since I know they will. If you're not a broadcast major like me, you can still get creative. Post pictures of you at internships and volunteer opportunities and explain what you did. Upload projects and papers that impacted you. Get creative and show who you really are.

3) Clean up the social media

Social media is a huge part of our society today. My grandma even uses Facebook and Instagram. It's so easy to want to post-beach day bikini pictures or photos from your 21st birthday outing, but the thing is, these employers don't know you personally. Their first impression of you could be your Facebook profile. An excellent way to give off a professional impression is to create a LinkedIn account. I did not create one until my senior year of college, and I wish I knew about it sooner. LinkedIn allows you to connect with businesses; the employers and employees. You have a profile picture but it allows you to show off your resume, courses taken, projects, recommendation letters, and much more.

4) Business cards

You never know who you could meet. You could be waitressing on the weekends during college and meet a CEO for a hospital who just so happens to have a paid internship opportunity open in your area of study. You pull out a business card from your apron and exchange contact info with him. Five years down the road, that internship turns into a job all because you were prepared. I realized how professional it looked to have business cards on you at all times. I keep some just about everywhere. You can put the link to your online portfolio, your email, cell number, and desired career. An inexpensive way to design your own business cards and get the most for your money is Vistaprint.com. Putting a picture on your card also is a way to stand out and allow them to connect a name on a card with a face.

5) Professional Wardrobe

I am still changing my style and going through my closet. There's nothing wrong with keeping up with the latest trends and styles but there is an issue when what you wear does not reflect who you want to be. If you want to be a marketing assistant, you will most likely be working in an office all day. You'll probably be wearing dresses, skirts, and pants inside the office. If you show up to work in your favorite pair of leggings with Converse and a crop top, I don't think your director would be too happy. I'm not telling you to wear a dress or dress pants everyday of your life. I am saying to start building your wardrobe now. Stop buying pieces of clothing you won't be able to wear after you graduate. Yes, definitely have some outfits you can go out with friends in or wear on a date. Keep your comfy leggings and oversized T-shirts. Don't be afraid to dress to impress now. My best friend from high school really instilled this in my mind. She began dressing more professional for classes and even when we would catch up over dinner. She integrated her love for style with clothes that fit her body right and make her look amazing. You can still look "appealing" without wearing things that leave little to the imagination. Dressing to impress not only allows you to feel confident about yourself but it allows you to leave a good impression on someone you may meet while out and about. Don't feel like you have to start freshmen year of college wearing dress pants and a blazer but don't forget to start building your wardrobe for post-graduation.

What if I don't know?

It's okay to start college and have no idea what you want to major in or do with that major. There are very broad majors you can get a degree in and use for a number of careers. But first, I want you to think about yourself. Be selfish for a second: What are your hobbies? What do you find joy in doing? What kind of people do you like to be around?

Whatever you choose to do, do not choose a major to make your parents happy. Choose it because it's right for YOU. Don't follow the misconception that ALL women are meant to be a stay at home mom or work part-time jobs. If you enjoy engineering and construction, do it. If you enjoy art and photography, do it. You can be a musician, chemist, doctor, fashion designer, business owner, teacher, and so much more. We need more women who will step up and believe that they can reach their dreams. You can be a CEO of a major corporation. You can be a surgeon. You can open your own wedding planning business. You can do whatever you are called to do in life. Yes, our parents know us better than anyone else. Only God knows what's truly best for you so seek Him, do your research, and seek the counsel of a career services department at your university. Most career service departments offer quizzes you can take to help you decide. Like I said before, the only way to know if you will truly enjoy a job is when you are out in the real world observing or working hands on. My entire life I was dead set on becoming a teacher. I had a chalkboard and world map in my room. I had a few students: my American Girl dolls, Polly Pocket, and my brother. When I started North Greenville University, I had to take an "Intro to Education" course, which involved observation at a local elementary school. After week three of observing, I knew it wasn't for me. Teachers are so great and change lives, but I knew there was something else out there I was made to do. I found Broadcast Media was a better fit for my personality and offered a large range of careers to choose from. I changed to Broadcast Media my sophomore year, and I knew it was the perfect fit. If you are not sure what you want to do specifically, research different jobs and see what major is required. Communications, business, and human resources are all safe choices because they make you into a well-rounded candidate. With those degrees, you could do event planning for a charity, become a wedding planner, manage public relations for a corporation, marketing for the New York Yankees, or even open your own boutique. There're endless possibilities. It's all about getting internships, filling your electives up with a variety of classes, and getting out there to meet new people.

Challenge:

What are some things you could put on a resume?

What jobs have you had in the past or currently?

Do you think there are some things you should delete on your social media? Why? Are there things in your wardrobe you know would make you look less appealing by employers?

Share your thoughts #GGC
www.gabyfanelli.com

Journal

Chapter 11
Mom

For the last chapter of this book, I thought I'd write about the most influential person in my life. It's funny how girls go through different phases with their mom. As a little girl, you go everywhere with mom, and you are proud. If mom went to the grocery store, you better believe I was by her side holding onto that shopping cart. Every night she would tell me how smart and special I was. She was my best friend. As a pre-teen, you start to get smelly and weird. You go through puberty. Mom gives you awkward talks and teaches you how to start taking care of yourself as a woman. I began to notice boys and would tell her all about my secret crush. Sometimes I would come home from school in tears because I was bullied. I remember how my mom seemed to hurt more than I did when she found out. Mom was my advocate. She stood up for me. She packed my lunch. She drove me all over the world before I had a car. She made sure I was in church every Sunday morning, Sunday night, and Wednesday night. When I was a teenager, I formed that "attitude" teenagers can form. Mom says she thinks someone else took over my body. My mom used to be my best friend. She never bullied me or called me fat. She was always there. She wiped my tears and packed my lunch. She and my dad sacrificed and still sacrifice money to buy my brother and me everything we could ever want or need. Somehow I forgot how much she did. I changed. I went my own way, and it didn't matter what she said not to do, I was fourteen, so I believed I was old enough to make my own choices. I was drinking, smoking, and allowing guys to take advantage of me. Now I look at 14-year-olds and see how young I really was. I hated church, and I was tired of hearing the sermons about everything I shouldn't do because "The Bible says so". My boyfriend at the time was not a Christian and did not care about God. He made me feel wanted and special because I didn't believe I was worth anything. During this time, my mom found out every single thing I had done. My best friend in 9th grade told on me. Cool, I know. NOT. But God had a plan. I hated my mom so bad during this time, and I even told her I hated her on Mother's day of that year. I broke her heart as well as my dad's heart. I was no longer their sweet innocent little girl. I was broken and hurting. She took away my phone. She deleted my social media. She didn't let me hang out with any friends. No more sleepovers and no more boyfriend. I was grounded for eight months. During this time something happened. All I had was church and my family. My mom did a study with me called Confident, and it rocked my world. I began to find my true identity, as I got involved in church. I learned I needed to forgive myself, and I learned God was pursuing me through that time. He wasn't going to let the devil have me. He knows I am only from the dust of the ground but says I am precious, valued, and important. I realized I liked to sing and became the worship leader for my youth group. I decided I wanted to help other girls with their insecurities too, so I designed a 1-day camp to help middle school girls to get outside of the box. I then was given the opportunity the summer before I left for college to lead the God Confident series to a group of middle and high school girls in my youth group. I realized I get a "high" from encouraging women, so I still to this day love to find ways to make my friends smile through random notes of encouragement or flowers. I say all of this to you so you will know how much my mom means to me and how much your mom cares for you. I am so glad my friend told on me. I'm glad my mom loved me so much that she grounded me. Before I left for college, I actually thanked her for doing that! Sometimes we don't understand at the moment why our moms are so concerned with our choices. They can seem controlling and suffocating. Why can't they just let us grow up when we go to college and become our own person, right? As I write this book, I am a senior in college, and my mom is my best friend. To this day when I call her crying, she cries with me. She sets me straight when I know I'm in the wrong. Girls can sometimes have twisted intentions and do things, so you look bad or fail. I know whatever I tell my mom is between us. I know she isn't going to spread my mistakes. The times I pushed my mom away, wanted to grow up, and do my own thing, I realize she always had my best interest in mind. I found out all those bad choices I made in high school, my mom made the same ones too. Mothers aren't trying to ruin our lives and nag us until we poke out our eyes. They were young too. Moms were invited to that crazy out-of-control party. Moms were offered marijuana and other drugs. They had their heart broken, and they broke some hearts. They gossiped and were gossiped about. They had things they didn't like about themselves. They wanted to look hot and get a guys attention too. They brought us into this world, and their God-given job is to make sure we feel beautiful, loved, and important. Do not take your mom for granted because when it's all said and done, friends always come and go. Mom is in your life until God takes her home.

Maybe you don't have a good relationship with your mom, or maybe you don't have a mom at all. Who is the person currently caring for you? (Your grandma, aunt, dad, older sibling) Maybe this chapter is challenging you to find a mother-figure to be there for you. A woman you can confide in and trust with your heart. Tell your mom you love her today and don't be afraid to be open with her. She might share that she too had or has the same struggles as you and if not, she still knows just what to do to get you through your journey.

Challenge:

How is your relationship with your mom or your mother-figure?

Who is someone you can adopt as your mother-figure if you don't have one?

How open are you with her?

If your mom knew some of the things you have done, would she freak out?

What are ways you can show your mom you appreciate her?

Share your thoughts #GGC
www.gabywrites.com

Journal

I would love to hear your college stories, life hacks, and personal thoughts about my book! Visit _www.gabywrites. com_ to connect with me and receive free printable resources, watch instructional videos, and gain access to my personal blog. I pray your college years are the most amazing time of your life.